MERLIN'S GUIDE TO
MYTHICAL CREATURES
FROM MANY LANDS

MERLIN'S GUIDE TO MYTHICAL CREATURES FROM MANY LANDS

A MYTHICAL CREATURE GUIDE FOR KIDS

BY ZACHARY HAMBY

ILLUSTRATED BY ZACHARY HAMBY
AND LUKE HAMBY

DEDICATION

For Rachel, Luke, and Jane

"Fantasy is hardly an escape from reality.
It's a way of understanding it."

–Lloyd Alexander–

"People who deny the existence of dragons are often
eaten by dragons. From within."

–Ursula K. Le Guin–

ISBN-10: 0-9827049-9-2
ISBN-13: 978-0-9827049-9-8

Merlin's Guide to Mythical Creatures from Many Lands
Written by Zachary Hamby
Illustrated by Zachary Hamby and Luke Hamby
Edited by Rachel Hamby
Published by Creative English Teacher Press in the United States
of America
Copyright © 2023 Creative English Teacher Press

TABLE OF CONTENTS

FOREWORD

Greetings! Merlin the Wizard here. Perhaps you have heard of me? I'm mainly known for my magic, and, of course, there was that whole business with the Sword in the Stone, King Arthur, and the Knights of the Round Table. But I will let you in on a little secret—my true passion has always been the study of **mythical creatures**.

It all started when I was but a lad, and I had to save my life by unearthing a couple of sleeping, subterranean dragons. (It's a long story.) That was my first experience with the thrill of discovering magical creatures. If I'd had my choice, I would have made a career out of it, but I had a higher calling. I left all that behind to raise King Arthur, help him set up his court at Camelot, and keep him from ruining everything. He really was quite helpless without me, you know.

After my illustrious career in politics, I decided to retire. Sure, sure, some people will tell you that I was sealed up in a cave by a beautiful enchantress. To be fair, this is what she thought she was doing. But frankly, I needed a break. So I slipped out the back and have been off adventuring ever since.

I have traveled the world (and a bit through time and space) to discover every magical creature I can. I have explored jungles, pyramids, frozen mountains, the darkest caves, and even New Jersey swamps to track down the creatures of myth and legend. And, if I do say so myself, I have been highly successful.

Now after years of creature-hunting, I'm ready to share this information with you. You, too, can know every wart and whisker of these wonderful beings. I'm putting it all in the capable hands of this author. I will still pop in from time to time with my own notes. (After all, you can't leave it to someone non-magical to get all the facts right.) It's *your* turn to discover these marvelous creatures for yourself. Happy hunting!

MAGICALLY YOURS,

Merlin

INTRODUCTION

Our world is full of creatures that climb, burrow, soar, and slither. They have marvelous features like shells and scales, tentacles and tails, wings and webbed toes. But what about those creatures even more amazing than the ones in our everyday world? Those hidden beasts and monsters that live on the edge of our imagination, just beyond what we think is possible? These mythical creatures look like nothing we've ever seen, and they can do things we only dream about. Some of them are combinations of ordinary creatures, and some are even a mixture of humans and beasts. Some are dark and frightening—ones you could imagine lurking in the depths of a nightmare, while others are whimsical and wondrous. In this book, you will discover them one by one, learn their histories, and unearth their secrets.

These creatures are called "mythical" because they only exist in the imagination, but this doesn't mean they aren't valuable to study. They represent the hopes and fears of people from all around the world and from across time.

Several of these creatures will take you back to the beginning of recorded history, when people reported seeing them in the ancient world. Others are a little more modern and may come from places much closer to home!

As you read, you'll find profiles filled with facts on each creature—along with its description, so you will be able to identify the creature when you see it. Also look for these symbols that showcase even more information about the creatures.

MERLIN MEMO This is a note from the master magician himself, giving you a little helpful background on the creature and maybe some advice for how to confront it.

CREATURE CONNECTION This is a fun fact or a description of how a certain creature relates to another.

MONSTER MESSAGE This is a message straight from the creature's mouth.

You'll find the beasts grouped into categories, but explore the guidebook in your own way. It's your journey to take! At the back, you'll also find an index to look up any creature by name.

Banshees, dragons, werewolves, and wendigos—a world full of creatures is waiting to be discovered! Your adventure is about to begin!

MERLIN MEMO "Imaginary" creatures indeed! Oh, you non-magical types! What do they teach you in those so-called schools? Well, the author certainly tried his best, but I think we can all agree that my introduction was better. Hopefully, he does better from here on out. (I'm not going to hold my breath.)

CREATURES FROM THE CLASSICAL WORLD

From the earliest moments of human history, people have told tales of fantastic creatures— tales so ancient that they have become the stuff of myth and legend. Today you can see references to these creatures everywhere—in books, films, artwork, and even video games. So keep your eyes open! You are bound to recognize a few of these classical creatures.

MERLIN MEMO There aren't many places that are "before my time," but ancient Greece is one. After riddling with the Sphinx, laboring through the Labyrinth, and staring down a few gorgons, I was able to drum up the information I needed.

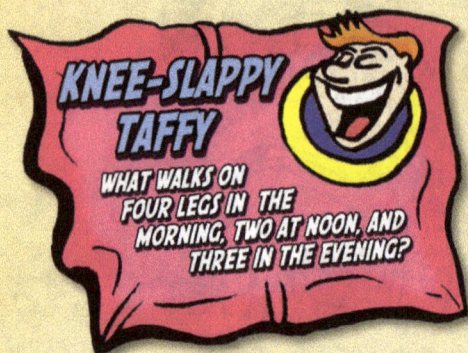

KNEE-SLAPPY TAFFY

WHAT WALKS ON FOUR LEGS IN THE MORNING, TWO AT NOON, AND THREE IN THE EVENING?

THE SPHINX HAD ME COMPLETELY STUMPED UNTIL I CLEVERLY DISCOVERED THE ANSWER TO HER LITTLE RIDDLE.

USING SOME GOLDEN THREAD, A PRINCESS NAMED ARIADNE WAS KIND ENOUGH TO HELP ME THROUGH THE LABYRINTH. IT WAS A BEAST—OR HOME TO ONE ANYWAY!

YOU ARE HERE

BASILISK
(BAZ-UH-LISK)

LOCATION: THE DESERT REGIONS OF THE MIDDLE EAST

DANGER RATING: 💀💀💀💀💀💀

Often called the King of the Reptiles, the basilisk is a monster with the head and body of a rooster and the tail of the snake. It looks so funny that you might laugh, but you'll be fleeing in terror once you hear about its deadly powers. A basilisk's gaze turns any living thing to stone, and its venomous touch kills its victims instantly. Its poisonous breath wilts flowers and plants, and the basilisk's acidic scales and feathers can shatter rocks with just the slightest touch. Whenever other serpents hear the basilisk's hiss, they slither away. So follow their lead!

Where does such a horrible creature come from? According to adventurers who have discovered the truth and lived to tell about it, a basilisk's birth defies nature. First, a rooster lays a rancid egg (an unnatural

feat for a male chicken) and buries it in a pile of dung. Drawn to the vile stench, a poisonous toad crawls onto the egg and warms it with its slimy belly. Weeks later, the egg cracks, and the basilisk breaks out!

MERLIN MEMO As invincible as it seems, a basilisk has weaknesses. Showing a basilisk a mirror and reflecting its gaze back at it will kill it. For this reason, some travelers carry a reflective crystal for extra protection. And if you release a weasel into a basilisk's den, the scent causes the basilisk to retreat—allowing the weasel to attack it with its teeth. So when faced with a basilisk, remember this handy tip: "Stop and reflect. There's still a way to *weasel* your way out of death."

CENTAUR
(SEHN-TAR)

LOCATION: THESSALY, GREECE

DANGER RATING: 💀💀💀

Half-man and half-horse, centaurs are famous for their strength and savagery. They make formidable enemies, so don't get on their bad side! Unfortunately, centaurs have horrible tempers, and that's easy to do. A constant war rages inside of them—a struggle between their human reasoning and their beastlike urges. Centaurs are known for starting fights, destroying property, and abducting women. According to one Greek myth, a wedding feast once ended badly when the centaurs tried to run away with the bride. You might want to leave them off the guest list for your next birthday party.

As one myth goes, a group of centaurs tried to take on Hercules, the mighty Greek hero. He was at a banquet when a rowdy gang of centaurs started a brawl. The centaurs stomped and raged, but Hercules won the fight, of course—he was the strongest man who ever lived.

But not all centaurs are crazed, wild brutes. One of the centaurs, **CHIRON**, was a wise teacher who trained many famous heroes, including Hercules, but he was badly wounded during a fight between Hercules and the other centaurs. In honor of Chiron's wisdom, the god Zeus placed him in the night sky as a constellation. You can still see him there today in the twinkling stars—a centaur drawing back his bow.

MERLIN MEMO If a centaur challenges you, remember that they attack with their front hooves. One good kick could crack your skull! So duck under their kicks, punch them in their horsey gut, and make them "hoof it" out of there.

CHIMERA
(KY-MEE-RUH)

LOCATION: LYCIA, MODERN-DAY TURKEY

DANGER RATING: 💀💀💀💀💀

There isn't a more confusing combination of creatures than the Chimera, which has three heads—that of a lion, a goat, and a snake—and the furry body of a lion. Not only is the Chimera's three-headed look frightening, but she also breathes fire! The Chimera's monster career began when she went on a killing spree—roasting travelers alive in the Lycian countryside for months, and it seemed that nothing could ever stop her.

Enter the the Greek hero, Bellerophon. Flying high over the Chimera's fiery breath on his winged horse, **PEGASUS**, Bellerophon affixed a lump of lead to the end of his spear and jabbed it down the beast's throat. It was a simple trick, but it worked! The lead melted in the Chimera's throat, stifling her fire and suffocating her. In modern times, the term *chimera* means something that can exist in your imagination but not in real life. Tell that to Bellerophon and Pegasus!

CREATURE CONNECTION The Chimera's father was **TYPHON**, a monster with a hundred fire-breathing snake heads, and her mother was **ECHIDNA**, a creature who was half woman and half serpent. The Chimera is also the sister of many other famous monsters in this guidebook, like the Sphinx (page 29), Cerberus (page 109), and Scylla (page 43). Talk about a freaky family!

MERLIN MEMO This critter is a nasty customer! You might have heard two heads are better than one, but three heads are just awful. If you plan to tangle with the Chimera, take along a lump of lead and a lot of courage!

CYCLOPS
(SY-KLOPS)

LOCATION: MOUNT OLYMPUS, GREECE

DANGER RATING: 💀💀💀

Cyclopes are towering giants with a single eye peering out from the middle of their forehead. Born at the beginning of time, cyclopes are the children of Uranus (Father Heaven) and Gaea

(Mother Earth), but their parents considered them so repulsive that they chained them up in the Under-world. Zeus, the king of the Greek gods, freed them so they could help him in his war against the Titans, and in return, the cyclopes forged him a mighty new weap-on—the thunderbolt. Cyclopes were also credited with building monuments in ancient Greece far too massive for any human to build.

But not all cyclopes were helpful! The most famous cyclops is **POLYPHEMUS**, who was a shepherd on an island in the middle of the Mediterranean Sea. When a hero named Odysseus and his crew landed on his is-land, Polyphemus trapped them inside his cave and ate them, one by one, until Odysseus crafted a giant stake and poked out Polyphemus's eye.

Some skeptics think that cyclopes were made up when ancient people discovered an elephant skull for the first time. The large hole in the middle of its head looks like an eye-socket, but it's really where the ele-phant's trunk attaches to its face.

MONSTER MESSAGE WHAT AM I SUPPOSED TO DO WHEN A BUNCH OF TASTY HUMANS SNEAK INTO MY CAVE AND EAT UP ALL OF MY FOOD? THEY'RE THE MONSTERS, NOT ME! THEY WERE SO UNGRATEFUL. THEY LEFT ME BLIND AND STOLE MY SHEEP. NOBODY GETS AWAY WITH THAT!

−POLYPHEMUS THE CYCLOPS−

GORGON

(GOR-GUN)

LOCATION: AEOLIA, MODERN-DAY TURKEY

DANGER RATING: 💀💀💀💀💀

I f you meet a gorgon, look away, or it'll be the last mistake you ever make! One glance from a gorgon's eyes will turn any creature into stone. Gorgon hair is made of writhing snakes, their eyes blaze with fire, and their tusk-like fangs drip blood. Even if gorgons don't get you with their petrifying stare, their ferocious bronze claws can rip you to shreds. Some say that gorgons have golden wings, but most people can't take a second glance to find out.

The most famous gorgon was **MEDUSA**. According to ancient Greek myth, Medusa was once a beautiful maiden who caught the eye of the sea god, Poseidon, but their love offended the goddess Athena, and she turned Medusa into the first gorgon. When Medusa's sisters pled their case to Athena, she transformed them into gorgons, too. The three Gorgons were banished to the edge of the world, and they killed anyone who ventured near. Medusa was slain by the hero Perseus, who used Medusa's severed head to turn his enemies into stone. Athena eventually placed the head in her shield, a reminder to everyone not to mess with the battle goddess. Mortals followed suit by painting a gorgon's face on their city walls, hoping that the sight of it would freeze their enemies in their tracks!

MONSTER MESSAGE *MEDUSA HERE! THIS BOOK RE-FLECTS BADLY ON ME! I DIDN'T ASK TO BE A MONSTER! POSEIDON CORNERED ME IN ATHENA'S TEMPLE. THEN ATHENA SHOWED UP, GOT THE WRONG IDEA, AND SUDDENLY I'M CURSED FOREVER! WHEN PEOPLE SAY I'M A HEARTLESS MONSTER, I SAY, "LOOK ME IN THE FACE AND TELL ME THAT." YOU KNOW, MY BIGGEST REGRET IS—*

(THE REST OF MEDUSA'S COMMENTS WERE LOST. THE INTERVIEWER ACCIDENTALLY LOOKED HER IN THE EYE.)

MANTICORE
(MANT-UH-KOR)

LOCATION: PERSIA

DANGER RATING: 💀💀💀💀

The Manticore arches its shaggy, lion back, draws its scorpion tail up into the air, and uses its keen human eyes to take aim at the man fleeing into the distance. Shoom! The tail launches a stinging dart, and the man falls down to the ground—his body convulsing as the dart's venom ends his life. The Manticore purrs to itself, "Dinnertime."

The Manticore is a beast with the body of a lion, the stinging tail of a scorpion, and the face of a human. You might think that since it has a human face, it would be friendly to our species. Think again! Manticore means "man-eater," which is exactly what the Manticore loves to do. Although it preys on many creatures, human flesh is its favorite. To trap its quarry, the Manticore can mimic human speech. So if you hear a friendly voice beckoning you from the desert underbrush, don't investigate! It might be the Manticore trying to lure you closer for the kill.

The Manticore is deadly both close and at a distance. It has six rows of teeth (three on the top jaw and three on the bottom), which can flay you alive, and its scorpion tail can shoot poisonous spikes with deadly accuracy.

MERLIN MEMO There is a rumor that the Manticore is just a normal, old tiger—nothing supernatural. But the Manticore probably started that rumor itself to put people off their guard. After all, it has *lyin'* in its blood.

MINOTAUR
(MIN-O-TAR)

LOCATION: THE LABYRINTH, THE ISLAND OF CRETE

DANGER RATING: 💀💀💀💀

If you're ever lost in an underground maze, and you hear a distant roar in the darkness, you'd better run for your life, because the Minotaur might be hot on your heels. The Minotaur has the body of a man and the head of a bull. His mother was the Queen of

Crete, and his father was a bull. The less said about that the better, but people love to gossip. As the mythical gossip goes, the queen was cursed by the sea god Poseidon and fell in love with the bull.

When Minos, the King of Crete, found out his wife gave birth to a bull-baby, he was horrified. He commanded the famously creative inventor Daedalus to build a subterranean maze, an inescapable network of twists and turns, that he called the Labyrinth. Then he dropped his newly born "step-son" monster into it. Whenever people ticked King Minos off, he simply tossed them in too, and the Minotaur took care of the rest. Roughly translated, "Minotaur" means the "bull of Minos."

Years later, when a group of young Greeks was dropped into the Labyrinth, a hero named Theseus killed the Minotaur and escaped—leaving King Minos bull-less.

 **MERLIN MEMO** If you want to tour the Labyrinth, you'll need the right gear to defeat the Minotaur. Bring a golden crown of light to see your way in the darkness. Make sure you have a sword as sharp as the horns of the Minotaur. Take a spool of thread to unwind as you travel the Labyrinth, and then follow it back to the entrance after you defeat the Minotaur. It worked for Theseus, and it'll work for you!

SATYR

(SAY-TER)

LOCATION: GREECE

DANGER RATING: 💀

Satyrs are jolly creatures with the haunches of a goat, the top half of a human, and goat-like horns and ears. They spend most of their time in the forests of Greece—dancing in the tall grass, playing their reed pipes, and chasing nature spirits called **NYMPHS**. These chases are their favorite pastime. Satyrs' goat legs are speedy, and most nymphs narrowly escape their embraces by transforming into a tree or a stream at the last minute—leaving their goaty admirers bleating up the wrong tree.

Typically, satyrs are afraid or wary of humans, so don't be surprised if they scatter when they see you. But be careful! If they get angry, they have been known to head butt, just like a goat, but with a lot more power. They're mostly fun-loving creatures though. As the original party animals, satyrs love the wild and crazy celebrations hosted by Dionysus, the Greek god of wine and revelry. Those shaggy legs can dance all night!

The first of all the satyrs is **PAN**, who was also the god of the woodlands. He invented the first set of reed pipes when he was chasing a nymph, and she turned herself into a reed to escape him. Just to prove a point, Pan uprooted her and whittled her into the musical instrument we still call a "pan flute" today.

 **CREATURE CONNECTION** Although satyrs got their start in ancient Greece, the Romans called satyrs **FAUNS**—like Mr. Tumnus of Narnia from *The Lion, the Witch, and the Wardrobe*.

SPHINX

(SFEENX)

LOCATION: THEBES, GREECE

DANGER RATING: 💀💀

What walks on four legs, flies on two wings, and asks the deadliest riddles around? If you guessed the Sphinx, you can live...for now. The Sphinx has the head of a woman and the body of a lion—not to mention the wings of an eagle and the tail of a snake. The only thing she likes more than a good riddle is a tasty human snack.

The original Sphinx was sent by the goddess Hera to torture the Greek city of Thebes. Anyone who passed on the road had to answer the Sphinx's riddle: "What walks on four legs in the morning, two legs at noon, and three legs in the evening?"

If travelers could not answer the riddle, the Sphinx would devour them. Finally, a hero named Oedipus came along, and he happened to guess the answer to the riddle: a mortal man. A man crawls on "four legs" as a baby, walks on two legs in the middle of life, and then uses two legs and a cane ("three legs") when he is old. The Sphinx was so enraged that Oedipus guessed her riddle, she leapt from a cliff and died.

CREATURE CONNECTION The Egyptians have their own version of the Sphinx, but he has a man's head on a lion's body and is a kindly protector of the dead, instead of a riddle-posing man-eater. The Egyptian monument (and wonder of the ancient world) called the Great Sphinx honors Egypt's version this beast. However, in a surprising twist, this man-lion combo is much closer to the Manticore (page 23) than the Sphinx.

CREATURES OF THE WAVES

The oceans are deep and mysterious, and we've only discovered a fraction of their secrets. Just when we think we've seen all the seas have to offer, something unfathomable rises from the depths and challenges everything we know to be true. These watery creatures, driven to the surface by either curiosity or appetite, interact with us land-dwellers in both thrilling and chilling ways. So read carefully because your next swim could bring you face to face with a kindly friend or a deadly foe!

MERLIN MEMO I knew I needed to plumb the deepest parts of the oceans if I were going to locate some of the world's most elusive creatures, so I enlisted the help of my old friend, Jules Verne himself to design a submersible fit for deep-sea exploration. I didn't quite travel 20,000 leagues under the sea, but apart from the Kraken taking a crack at me, the whole thing went swimmingly.

I ASKED NESSIE IF I COULD HAVE ONE OF HER SCALES. SHE SAID, "SURE! NO SKIN OFF MY BACK!"

A MERMAID GAVE ME HER BELT. SHE DIDN'T WANT IT ANYWAY. IT DIDN'T MATCH HER SHOES.

MERLIN

A KAPPA TRIED TO TRAP ME, BUT I STAYED AS COOL AS A CUCUMBER.

KAPPA

(KAP-UH)

LOCATION: JAPAN

DANGER RATING: 💀💀💀

The kappa, one of Japan's trickiest monsters, resembles a furless, frog-skinned monkey with webbed fingers and toes, the shell of a turtle, and a strange little cup-shaped hole on the top of its skull. Kappas terrorize Japan's rivers and lakes by luring unsuspecting people into the water, drowning them, and then drinking their blood. Luckily, there is one thing that kappas love more than human blood: cucumbers. If a family writes their last name on a cucumber and flings it into the waters where the kappa lives, it's said that the monster will accept this veggie sacrifice and spare all of the members of that family.

When looking for prey, kappas also like to wander from their watery homes. In order to safely leave their ponds and lakes, they must fill their funny little skull cup with water to sustain them while they are away. So, if you encounter a kappa, simply bow to it to show respect. It will do the same, and when it does, the water will spill out of its skull cup. The kappa will have to flee back to its watery dwelling immediately or shrivel up and die from dehydration.

MERLIN MEMO There's also a rumor that kappas are repelled by flatulence. So if all else fails, let out a toot, and the kappa will scoot!

CREATURE CONNECTION In the *Harry Potter* books, **GRINDYLOWS** are an English version of kappas that appear in the lake near Hogwarts. They use their spindly arms to drag victims down into the water when they come too close. So if you see a grindylow, remember this tip: "Turn around! Don't drown!"

KELPIE

(KEL-PEE)

LOCATION: SCOTLAND AND IRELAND

DANGER RATING: 💀💀💀

You're out for an early morning walk when you spy the most beautiful horse you've ever seen standing in the shallows of a lake. Its hide is glistening, and its mane is flowing in the breeze. It seems tame, so maybe it's just lost. It lowers its head kindly, almost as if it's inviting you to climb onto its back and take a ride. But rider beware! You've just encountered a deadly water kelpie. If you were to climb on, you would find yourself magically stuck to its back, and no amount of tugging will be able to free you. With you aboard, the kelpie will run nimbly across the surface of the water before plunging beneath the waves—ending the ride of your life by drowning you and then feasting on your flesh. Kelpies can even drown whole groups of victims, because no matter how many riders mount it, the kelpie's back will stretch and stretch to hold them all. On this deadly ride, the more, the merrier.

Kelpies come from the realm of the fairies (pg. 51) and they also possess the power to shapeshift. Kelpies can appear as handsome young men wandering the shoreline, crying to themselves. Their goal is to lure curious young girls into their world because if a kelpie's tear is absorbed into a human's skin, the human becomes its slave forever.

 **MERLIN MEMO** If you see a strange horse offering you a ride, just say, "Nay!" If you're not sure, look closely for the truth: A kelpie's hooves face backward instead of forward, and no matter whether it's in human or horse form, a kelpie will have a bit of seaweed woven into its hair or mane.

KRAKEN
(CRACK-UN)

LOCATION: OFF THE COAST OF NORWAY

DANGER RATING: 💀💀💀💀💀

I t's a fine, breezy day, and a ship is sailing smoothly along on a calm sea. Suddenly, innumerable tentacles rise from the waters and surround the ship, their suckers pulsing greedily. The Kraken has come to feed. As the crew scrambles for the lifeboats, the tentacles twine around the masts, snapping them like twigs. The sails crash down onto the fleeing sailors. The Kraken squeezes the remaining life out of the ship and drags it under. As quickly as it began, the struggle is over. The ship is gone, and only a few bubbles on the surface of the sea remain.

The Kraken is the deadliest of the sea creatures. First reported by Nordic sailors, it resembles a supersized squid or octopus and measures up to a mile and a half wide. When the Kraken rises to the surface, its body is so vast that it's often mistaken for an island.

As one story goes, a ship once sailed between the sleeping monster's jaws, thinking they were rocks jutting up from the water. But even the largest ships are no match for the Kraken. In 1782, when ten British warships disappeared, the Kraken was the prime suspect.

People thought stories of the Kraken were just a sailor's tale until a giant squid washed up on a beach. While some giant squid are 43 feet in length, as long as a school bus, they're nowhere near the size of the Kraken! Still they're proof that the ocean holds many secrets.

MERLIN MEMO If the Kraken attacks your ship, it's no time to be skittish toward your squid-ish foe. Avoid the tangle of tentacles, and aim your harpoon for the Kraken's eyes, the monster's only weak spot.

LOCH NESS MONSTER
(LOCK NES)

LOCATION: SCOTLAND

DANGER RATING: 💀

Deep down at the bottom of the famous Scottish lake lives the shy Loch Ness Monster. Nessie rarely travels to the surface, but when she does, her long neck and aquatic dinosaur flippers cause quite a stir! Witnesses usually see her rolling playfully around in the water or poking her head above water for just a second.

People have known that a wonderfully mysterious monster dwells in Loch Ness for 1,500 years. The ancient tribes of Scotland (called the Picts) revered all kinds of animals and carefully etched pictures of them onto tall, standing stones. All of the animals are easily identified except for one that's defied explanation for ages: a beast with a long muzzle and flippers instead of feet.

Only a few photographers have managed to snap a picture of Nessie. Her most famous moment occurred in 1934 when an English doctor took a photo called the "Surgeon's Photograph." In the grainy shot, you can just glimpse a shadowy neck and back lifting above the waves. For over sixty years, the picture was considered proof by many that Nessie really existed, but in time, it was discovered that the snapshot was a hoax. The "monster" was actually a plastic-and-wooden head attached to a toy submarine.

More recently, researchers tested Loch Ness for traces of reptile DNA. The tests came back negative, though they found plenty of eel DNA. Could Nessie actually be a giant eel? The hunt for the real Nessie continues!

MONSTER MESSAGE *EVERY TIME I TAKE A PEEK AT THE WORLD ABOVE THE WAVES, THERE'S SOMEONE THERE SNAPPING MY PICTURE! I KNOW I'M PHOTOGENIC, BUT CAN'T A MONSTER GET A LITTLE PRIVACY?*

—NESSIE—

MERMAID
(MER-MAID)

LOCATION: THE SEAS AND OCEANS OF THE WORLD

DANGER RATING: 💀

A silvery fish tail rises above the sea foam, beckoning you to come closer. But instead of a fish resting beneath the water, you see a girl's smiling face. You've just glimpsed a mermaid—a half-human, half-fish creature. Although playful at heart, mermaids can bring both good and bad fortune. They have been known to speak sweetly to lonely sailors, right before they drag them underwater to their deaths. On other occasions, they have saved whole shipwrecked crews from being lost in the waves.

Even though they are at home under the sea, some mermaids possess the ability to sprout legs and come ashore. They especially love attending fairs and festivals, where young men may not realize they are courting mermaids in disguise. Some humans marry mermaids—both on accident and on porpoise—I mean, purpose. Most seaside folk know that if you can capture a mermaid's cap or belt, you gain power over her.

Mermaids aren't the only merfolk, as mermen exist too, but they swim up to the surface much less often. Sailors blame mermen for stirring up violent storms at sea.

CREATURE CONNECTION The Greek myths tell of sea creatures called **SIRENS**, whose song hypnotizes sailors into leaping from their boats and swimming to their deaths. Though nobody knows exactly what sirens look like (because they leave no survivors!) many people imagine them to look like mermaids.

SCYLLA AND CHARYBDIS
(SIL-UH, KUH-RIB-DIS)

LOCATION: A STRAIT BETWEEN SICILY AND ITALY

DANGER RATING: 💀💀💀💀💀💀

f you happen to sail around the boot-tip of Italy, you will see the land on either side bottlenecking your ship into a narrow strait. Beware! Ahead, two monsters await you, each as deadly as the other.

You will have to face one of them though because it is impossible to avoid them both.

One is Scylla, a six-headed monster. Each of her heads is the face of a sharp-toothed woman on a long, snake-like neck, and her stomach is made up of snarling, gnashing dog heads. Her snake-like tail anchors her firmly to the cliff side. But don't let her stationary position fool you! Her long, serpentine necks allow her to gobble up any tasty humans who happen to sail by—just when they think they've made it safely past her.

When you sail away from her side, you run right into the clutches of the other monster, Charybdis. She will suck you down into her gigantic whirlpool-mouth and gelatinous belly. Then, she will belch whatever remains of you out again, spraying you high into the sky.

When the hero Odysseus was forced to sail through the strait, he chose to face Scylla instead of Charybdis. She immediately gobbled up six of his men (one for each head), but the rest of his crew survived. Talk about taking one for the team!

MERLIN MEMO If you're ever choosing between Scylla and Charybdis, choose Scylla because she's easier to fool. Bring a crew of stuffed dummies. She'll snatch up six of these dummies and leave you free to sail on. Don't choose Charybdis! She's a real drag!

CREATURES OF THE AIR

A shadow passes over the sun, and those of us with our feet on the ground look to the sky in awe, fear, and wonder. Soaring creatures rule a kingdom all their own. They are the masters of the air and the keepers of the rain, the thunder, and lighting. So when you are searching for mythical monsters, remember to look to the skies! You may be surprised what wondrous creatures soar above.

MERLIN MEMO Hot in pursuit of some winged wonders, I called up another old friend, Leonardo da Vinci, to see if I could try out one of his patented flying contraptions. Before you knew it, I was up, up, and away on a creature-chasing adventure in the sky! If only I wasn't so afraid of heights!

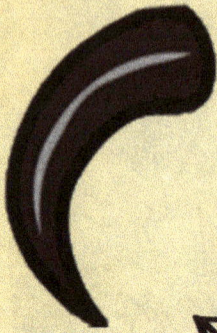

GRIFFIN CLAW: A GRIFFIN INVITED ME OVER FOR A MIDDAY SNACK—I MEAN, TO BE A MIDDAY SNACK. FORTUNATELY, I GAVE HIM A MANICURE AND ESCAPED.

I TRIED TO NAB A PHOENIX, BUT THE LITTLE BOOGER CRUMBLED INTO ASH. SO I JUST TOOK IT IN A TO-GO BAG.

I WAS GIVEN THIS LOVELY PEARL BY A KINDLY DRAGON IN THE REGION OF HUNAN. THE EUROPEAN DRAGONS DIDN'T GIVE ME ANYTHING EXCEPT SECOND-DEGREE BURNS.

DRAGON

(DRAH-GUN)

LOCATION: WORLDWIDE

DANGER RATING: 💀💀💀💀💀💀💀

With its leathery wings, fiery breath, glowing eyes, and deadly claws, the dragon is feared far and wide. In its lair, lit by smoldering snores, the dragon sleeps on great mounds of golden treasure. If even a single cup is stolen from its hoard, woe to the thief! The dragon awakes, and it takes to the sky, raining down fire and death over the countryside.

While this is the most famous type of dragon, many varieties exist all over the world, and in all shapes and sizes. They can be winged or wingless, legged or legless, and some slither along the ground like snakes. Some breathe forth clouds of poisonous gas, and others have acid for blood. You can find dragons in all kinds of places, too—flying through the sky, burrowing deep into the earth, or even swimming in rivers and seas.

Generally speaking, European dragons are dangerous and not to be trusted. But dragons from some Asian cultures can be kindly helpers to humanity, sending rains that irrigate the fields and help crops to grow. They fly without wings, have long moustaches, and receive their powers from lustrous pearls that grow upon their heads.

Over time, dragons have retreated further into the earth, so now only the most intrepid explorers possesses the courage and ingenuity to find them.

MERLIN MEMO When battling a beastly dragon, come prepared for fire by bringing your metal (not wooden!) shield, and when striking, aim for the dragon's soft underbelly. But when encountering a friendly dragon, bring a gift. It's only polite.

CREATURE CONNECTION Mesoamerican myths speak of a feathered serpent decorated with the bright feathers of a quetzal bird. In Toltec and Aztec traditions, this feathered serpent is **QUETZALCOATL**, or "bird-snake," a god who benefited humanity by inventing the Aztec calendar and teaching people to grow maize. And according to the K'iche' Maya people, a god appearing as a feathered serpent created the universe.

FAIRY

(FAIR-EE)

LOCATION: EUROPE

DANGER RATING: 💀

In the midst of a forest clearing, a cloud of sparkling beings six inches tall flutter in midair, their transparent wings glittering as they float and dance to hypnotic music. It is an enchanting sight, and you might want to join their merriment, but before you take another step, think twice. Humans who interrupt a fairy celebration often regret it.

Fairies are a perplexing lot, using their powers both for good and for evil. Fairies sometimes bring gifts to poor farmers, like corn and bread or toys for children, but other times they play horrible tricks, like curdling pails of milk or spattering mud over clean clothes hanging on the line. Fairy tricksters also carry away human babies in the night, leaving behind a fairy child called a changeling in their place.

You'll only spot fairies above ground, but they actually live underground in ancient graves called "fairy mounds," portals to the fairy world. Some humans have traveled there—either on purpose or through the fairy's tricks. Although it is a place filled with eternal beauty, feasting, and singing, mortals must be careful. If you eat any fairy food, you can never return to your own world. When you do return, even after a short visit, you will find that years have passed, even if it feels like only moments have gone by. If you spy a fairy ring, a circular growth of mushrooms or moss on the ground, do not step inside it, for it could be a portal to the fairy world!

CREATURE CONNECTION Another type of English fairies are **PIXIES**—like Tinkerbell from *Peter Pan*.

GRIFFIN
(GRIF-IN)

LOCATION: THE MIDDLE EAST AND CENTRAL ASIA

DANGER RATING: 💀💀

A dark mineshaft extends before you, and in the murky tunnel, you spot the bright glimmer of gold. It's exactly the treasure you have come for, but it isn't just there for the taking. Between you and the gold sits the griffin, the offspring of the king of the beasts and the king of the birds. Famous for guarding mines, griffins have the head and wings of an eagle and the furry body of a lion. Its eagle eyes glitter in the darkness as it soundlessly stalks you.

Most intruders don't stand a chance against the griffin's sharp talons and killer beak, which can cut through any armor. When they aren't using their talons to shred foes, they're digging for gold. Horses are a griffin's favorite prey, perhaps because many soldiers have attacked them on horseback. Horses gallop away as fast as they can from griffins, and you probably should, too.

On rare occasions, a griffin's hatred of horses turns to love, and a **HIPPOGRIFF** is born. It has the head and wings of a griffin and the body of a horse—just like Buckbeak from the *Harry Potter* books.

MERLIN MEMO Want to fight a griffin? Better not. But if you want to grab its gold, bait it with a bit of red meat. Then sneak into its hoard and pilfer some treasure. Don't get too greedy though—if the griffin finishes its snack too quickly, it will finish you!

CREATURE CONNECTION South American myths tell of the **ALICANTO**, a flightless bird that loves to gobble up precious metals like gold and silver. At night, its body glows the color of its latest meal. Treasure hunters follow it in hopes of making a lucky strike! But if the wily Alicanto catches on, it might change direction and lead its tracker off a cliff!

HARPY

(HAR-PEE)

LOCATION: GREECE

DANGER RATING: 💀💀

Harpies are filthy creatures with the head of a woman and the body of a buzzard, famous for swooping down on their victims with the fury of a thousand storms. Harpy means "snatcher" in Greek, and these foul fowls live up to the name. Their attacks were so common and deadly that in ancient Greece, any time someone disappeared without a trace, people said, "The harpies must have snatched them!"

Harpies are also known for their stench. Their odor can pollute anything they come near (just like some people's socks). In fact, the Greek god Zeus gave the harpies the job of tormenting Phineus, a mortal man who had annoyed him, and every day a beautiful banquet was magically laid out before Phineus. But before he could eat, the harpies swooped out of the sky, tore up the food with their beaks, and squirted their droppings onto the table, leaving Phineus to starve amidst his ruined feast. The harpies had such a reputation for doing Zeus's dirty work that they became known as the "Hounds of Zeus." So if you see a harpy, look out, for you might have offended someone very high up.

According to some adventurers, the harpies now live on a Mediterranean island, while others report that they prefer the Underworld, where they can torment souls all day long.

CREATURE CONNECTION Two of the fastest creatures ever born, the horses of the great warrior Achilles, were the children of the harpies. How do we know? They could run like the wind!

PEGASUS
(PEG-UH-SUS)

LOCATION: MOUNT OLYMPUS, GREECE

DANGER RATING: ☠

In olden days, young Greeks would sneak from their homes at night and make their way to a nearby bubbling spring, where they hoped to capture just a glimpse of the famous magical horse Pegasus, settling to earth with great sweeps of his majestic wings.

Pegasus was born when the hero Perseus severed Medusa's head (pg. 22), and the steed flew forth from her magical blood. Pegasus lived his life wild and free until a hero named Bellerophon captured him. With his winged mare, Bellerophon slew the multi-headed monster called the Chimera (page 17).

But the duo's partnership was short-lived. Bellerophon let his hero status go to his head and commanded Pegasus to fly him to the top of Mount Olympus to meet with the gods. But since the hero wasn't invited, Zeus sent a horsefly to sting Pegasus, causing the steed to buck his rider. Bellerophon survived his fall, but he never rode Pegasus again. Zeus welcomed Pegasus and gave him the job of transporting the god's mighty thunderbolts, which were crafted by the cyclopes (page 19). To this day, Pegasus appears as a constellation in the night sky.

MONSTER MESSAGE OKAY, HERE'S THE SCOOP—THIS BOOK SAYS THAT I THREW BELLEROPHON BECAUSE I WAS STUNG. HORSEFEATHERS! I KNEW HE WOULD TICK OFF ZEUS AND GET US BOTH KILLED, SO I BUCKED HIM OFF. ZEUS REWARDED ME WITH A STABLE ON MOUNT OLYMPUS. NOW, I EAT LIKE A HORSE AND LIVE FREE AS A BIRD!

—PEGASUS—

MERLIN MEMO If you want to catch a ride on Pegasus, he only drinks from certain watering holes—springs that he himself cut into the ground with a single strike of his magical hooves.

PHOENIX

(FEE-NIX)

LOCATION: EGYPT

DANGER RATING: 💀

eathers flickering like fire, the phoenix bird thoughtfully builds its nest. Using its golden beak, it carefully selects each twig and threads it skillfully through the others. As it builds, its feathers flicker faster, and it knows its time is close. It has lived for 500 years, but now it is time to die. Settling into its completed nest, the phoenix raises its head toward the sun and bursts into flames! The phoenix fans the blaze with its fiery wings until it engulfs its entire body. Then the bird crumbles into ash. It seems the scene is over, but there is a flash, a single spark springs up, and a new fire-red phoenix flies forth from the ashes.

The miracle of the phoenix's rebirth symbolizes life after death and the rising and setting of the sun. Although it is an astounding event, there are very few eyewitnesses to it, for there is only one phoenix in existence at a time, and each lives 500 years.

Since the phoenix is a symbol of regeneration, the city of Phoenix, Arizona was given its name because it was built on the ruins of a previous settlement.

CREATURE CONNECTION Though the first mention of the phoenix was made in Ancient Greece, many cultures have their own version of the phoenix. Egyptian myths call theirs the **BENNU**, a heron that regenerates itself like the rising sun, Chinese tales speak of the **FENG HUANG**, considered a messenger from heaven and a bringer of peace, and Russian stories talk of the **FIREBIRD**, with its precious feathers that glow like dancing flames.

THUNDERBIRD

(THUN-DER-BERD)

LOCATION: NORTH AMERICA

DANGER RATING: 💀💀

Swirling storm clouds conceal its massive wings, a deafening roar bursts from its beak, and as you squint up, you see flashes of lighting that silhouette its bared talons. You've just sighted a thunderbird.

Revered by many of the indigenous peoples of North America, a thunderbird is a giant eagle-like creature known for its storm-creating powers. With a wingspan the length of two canoes set tip to tip, a thunderbird travels in a covering of clouds and rain. Its flapping wings make the sound of thunder with each stroke, and its eyes flash lightning.

Yet as terrifying as they look, thunderbirds are defenders and helpers of earthbound people. Upon their backs, they bring the rains that water the plants and other vegetation. Leaders pray to thunderbirds for wisdom, and sometimes these majestic creatures transform and walk among men. As one myth goes, when floodwaters trapped a great indigenous chief on a mountaintop, a thunderbird took human form and rescued his people from being swept away.

Centuries ago, the thunderbirds fought a war against horned water serpents that wanted to flood the world and wipe out all human life. To preserve their human friends, the thunderbirds slew these monsters one by one. Even to this day, people say that a bolt of lightning is a horned serpent being hurled to the ground by a thunderbird's claws, and the resulting boom is the sound of its impact.

CREATURE CONNECTION The thunderbird is called a **ROC** in the Middle East. The roc is a giant white bird of prey large enough to scoop up an elephant in its talons.

CREATURES OF THE LAND

Secluded forest glens, glittering caves, and hidden mountain valleys are all places where creatures shield themselves from the prying eyes of the world. Here you will find creatures that go upon the land—the same as you and me. As you enter their domain, remember to proceed respectfully. This is their secret sanctuary, and even a kindly creature can be spooked by a rude intruder.

MERLIN MEMO Ah, Africa! First, I traded in my wizard robes for a safari outfit. As they say, "safari, so good!" After swapping stories with my old spider-pal, Anansi, I was off on a cross-country journey to locate as many of these "down-to-earth" creatures as I could. I *landed* quite a few of them!

ANANSI GAVE ME ONE OF HIS TREASURES—MY VERY OWN STORY!☀

I ALWAYS KEEP SOME LEPRECHAUN SPRAY ON HAND FOR WHEN I NEED TO GRAB A FEW OF THEIR LUCKY CHARMS.

LEPRECHAUN B-GONE

I FOUND THIS LITTLE LESHI SEEDLING ALONE IN THE FOREST. I THOUGHT I MIGHT RAISE HIM MYSELF. NOW HE'S GROWING LIKE A WEED.

ANANSI

(UH-NAHN-ZEE)

LOCATION: WEST AFRICA

DANGER RATING: 💀💀

With all the skills of a spider and the cunning mind of a man, Anansi is quite a creature. Seeing his eight arachnid arms and legs might be frightening, but he is one of the greatest benefactors of human beings. As one African saying goes, "The wisdom of Anansi is greater than that of all the world put together."

Using his spider-like legs, Anansi has woven a web-ladder into the heavens many times over, and each perilous climb he made was for the benefit of mankind. Back when there was no light in the world, he convinced the sky god to create the sun. When night remained dark, Anansi climbed again and asked the sky god to make the moon, fixing the problem of heavenly balance.

Many stories are told about Anansi—and rightfully so. Long ago, the sky god kept all the stories in the world to himself. The sky god said he would share his stories in exchange for four of the most dangerous creatures on the earth—Mmoboro the hornet swarm, Osebo the leopard, Onini the python, and Mmoatia the tricky fairy.

Clever Anansi sealed the hornets into a gourd, lured the leopard into a pit, tied the python to a branch, and trapped the fairy with a sap-covered doll. Anansi delivered these creatures and won stories for the world to enjoy. To this day, all wonderful tales in Africa are called "spider stories" in his honor.

MONSTER MESSAGE It's all true! I am the amazing spider man! Without me, you wouldn't have any of these stories—or light to read them by. Next time you go to smash a spider, think of how much this little spider did for you!

—ANANSI—

DWARF
(DWARF)

LOCATION: NORTHERN EUROPE

DANGER RATING: 💀

Deep in the earth, the forge fires are glowing hot, and the air is filled with the clanging sounds of hammers striking anvils. The dwarves of myth are hard at work crafting weapons and treasures that human minds can barely comprehend!

Dwarves, the mythological world's greatest crafts-men, are short and stocky creatures with long beards. Since a dwarf is fully grown at three years old and turns gray at age seven, most of them are mistaken for little, old men. Crabby and antisocial, they avoid other creatures when they can—preferring to live in the sprawling, subterranean palaces and cities they have brilliantly crafted underground. There they can keep to themselves—and work in their forges, which is what they love to do most. Some dwarves wear long, taper-ing caps that hang down their backs and allow their wearer to turn invisible. But most dwarf magic is re-served for the wonders they create: the greatest weapons and treasures known to humanity. Both the hammer of Thor, the Norse thunder god, and the spear of Odin, his father, are Dwarven-made™.

 **MERLIN MEMO** Although dwarves were the first creatures to teach humans the craft of metal-work, these days they are greedier with their gifts. So if you meet a dwarf, don't be dopey! Greet him in the proper dwarf fashion by saying, "May your beard never grow thin!" Then, just maybe, he'll share some of his treasures and knowledge with you.

MONSTER MESSAGE   *WANTED: KINDHEARTED PRINCESS WILLING TO SHARE A COTTAGE WITH SEV-EN UNWASHED, UNCULTURED, UNRULY ROOMMATES. IMMUNITY TO POISONED APPLES PREFERRED.*

— A. DWARF —

ELF
(ELF)

LOCATION: NORTHERN EUROPE

DANGER RATING: 💀

The house was a mess when you went to bed—dirty dishes everywhere, laundry piled high, and dust bunnies all over the floor. But then strange noises awake you in the middle of the night. You tip-toe downstairs to find your house full of activity. Little creatures are doing the dishes, scrubbing the laundry, and sweeping the floors. Elves have moved in!

Elves are small beings, no more than a foot high, with pointed ears, large eyes, and curly hair. Long ago, elves discovered that the houses of nearby villagers were far comfier than the forest they dwelled in. Building their homes within the walls of human houses, elves adopt a family and emerge at night to help with chores and tasks. But don't get your hopes up: Elves do not do homework!

Grateful families can leave a bowl of porridge or cream out each night to thank their miniature helpers. But never leave anything more—especially clothing, or the elves will be insulted and leave forever. The elves are a proud people and never take charity. They know how to make an exit, too! Before they vanish, they will break all the dishes, spill the milk, run the cows away, and spoil the crops.

CREATURE CONNECTION In England a household elf is called a **BROWNIE**, in Russia a **DOMOVOY**, and in Germany a **KOBOLD**. In the *Harry Potter* series, Dobby is part of a race called **HOUSE ELVES** that gain their freedom when they receive a gift of clothing from their masters. There are elves in *The Hobbit* and *The Lord of the Rings*, but they are a taller, more regal breed.

GIANT
(GY-ANT)

LOCATION: WORLDWIDE

DANGER RATING: 💀💀

Whether they're stepping over an entire field with a single stride, scooping up a herd of cattle for a midday snack, or guzzling a lake dry to wash it all down, giants are a menace to any kingdom! More than just humongous human beings, giants are an ancient race of creatures that range from 18 to hundreds of feet tall. They have potato-shaped noses, floppy ears, and faces usually covered with boils and blisters. Some have two or three heads—each uglier than the last. It's enough to make you die of fright! And dying is exactly what giants want you to do. One of their favorite dishes is stewed children, and they enjoy nothing more than a human heart properly seasoned with pepper and vinegar. Their huge noses can smell human blood from miles away: "Fee Fie Fo Fum! I smell the blood of an Englishman!" There is some magic in giants, but they are not very bright in using it. So instead, they prefer brute force.

For all these reasons, giants have been the enemies of good for centuries. A boy named Jack gained fame around England for his ability to whittle these enemies down to size (sometimes literally chopping them down!) As time has gone by, giants have become increasingly rare, and some people say they retreated into the clouds, so now it takes a magic beanstalk to even find one.

MERLIN MEMO In spite of all their evildoing, I'd like to say a kind word about (some) giants. It was a group of giants who helped me build England's massive stone structure, Stonehenge. This old back couldn't do all that heavy lifting!

GOBLIN

(GOB-LIN)

LOCATION: EUROPE

DANGER RATING: 💀💀

Standing knee high to a human, goblins are cruel creatures with greenish skin, bat-like ears, and glowing eyes. They love to nip and poke at their victims with their long fingernails, needle-like teeth, and jagged spears. Rowdy goblin gangs have been known to drag unsuspecting humans into their tunnels where they dwell in a cavernous kingdom and do the bidding of their goblin king. Long ago, the creatures of earth cursed all goblins to live underground because of their frightful faces and wicked hearts. If the light of the sun touches a goblin, its body will painfully petrify into stone.

Nighttime belongs to the goblins, and no home is safe from their mischief. Even if your door is bolted tight, goblins can slink through the tiniest crack. They are the source of all nightmares and love to sit on the chests of sleeping humans to trigger a frightful dream. They jolt their victims awake by yanking the bedsheets off or slapping them in the face. If you wake from a nasty nightmare, you might hear the laughter of a goblin as it escapes.

Goblins have another notorious weakness: their huge, floppy, and tender feet. So, if you encounter a goblin, stomp on its toes for all you're worth, and send it screaming back to its hole.

CREATURE CONNECTION An **IMP** is another name for a goblin, and a **HOBGOBLIN** is a less-menacing (but just as annoying) type. Rumpelstiltskin, the notorious baby-stealer, is thought to be a goblin. **REDCAPS** are a breed of goblins who wear iron boots and caps dyed with human blood. The fantasy author J.R.R. Tolkien called his goblins **ORCS**. In short: A goblin by any other name…still stinks!

GREMLIN

(GREHM-LIN)

LOCATION: GREAT BRITAIN

DANGER RATING: 💀💀

Flying high over the English Channel, a plane's engine splutters, its propellers stop, and it begins to nosedive toward the sea. The pilot barely manages to grab the radio and call out a frantic one-word message, "Gremlins!" before his plane crashes into the waves.

Thoroughly modern menaces, gremlins are little creatures between 12 and 20 inches tall that love to sabotage machinery—especially the equipment inside airplanes. In the years following World War I, pilots began to report seeing "little men" on the wings of their planes, tearing open machinery compartments, biting through wires, and shredding their planes apart piece by piece. Some pilots were so terrified, they even bailed out mid-flight! This terror continued into World War II, when Gremlins brought down planes fighting on both sides of the conflict.

Even as destructive as they are, gremlins are dapper dressers, often outfitted in trousers, jackets, spats, and top hats. Because airplane fuel is their drink of choice, they live in underground burrows near airfields. When a plane is taking off, the gremlins will jump aboard and tamper with it until it finally crashes. As the planes plummet toward the ground, gremlins jump free and land on their top hats, which are wonderful shock absorbers.

As technology has advanced over the years, so have gremlins. Even in the modern era, they still know how to throw a wrench in the works. So the next time your computer has a meltdown, you can bet that a gremlin has struck again!

LEPRECHAUN

(LEHP-REE-KAWN)

LOCATION: IRELAND

DANGER RATING: 💀

There's no mistaking leprechauns: little, bearded men wearing green waistcoats and breeches with bright buckles on their shoes. Famous for their pot of gold hidden at the end of the rainbow, these little people are the target of many treasure hunters. Those who catch a leprechaun can make it do whatever they ask. Some ask for three wishes. Others ask for the location of the pot of gold. But because of the little people's wily tricks, most leprechaun-catchers end up empty-handed.

Leprechauns are wealthy for a reason: They know how to hoard and keep their gold. Once a man caught a leprechaun and commanded him to reveal the location of his buried treasure. The leprechaun pointed to a perfectly ordinary bush in a field. Since the man did not have a shovel to dig, he tied a red ribbon around the bush to mark it until he could return with one. Knowing how tricky Leprechauns can be, the man commanded the Leprechaun not to remove the ribbon, and he agreed. The man hurried home, grabbed up a shovel, and returned only to find that every bush in the field now bore a red ribbon. As he howled in defeat, the distant sound of Leprechaun laughter reached his ears.

MERLIN MEMO Catching a leprechaun can be easier than you think! If you're walking through the woods, listen for the sound of tiny hammers. Leprechauns are fond of making shoes and spend their days making the finest ones around. When you spot the leprechaun, do not turn away. As long as you are looking at a leprechaun, it cannot use its magic to disappear. But if you turn your head, even for a split second, it will vanish.

LESHI
(LEE-SHEE)

LOCATION: RUSSIA AND OTHER SLAVIC COUNTRIES

DANGER RATING: 💀💀

Y ou are walking through the forest on a familiar path, headed for your home, when you realize the path is no longer there. The forest has changed, and trees bar your way on every side. Confused and frightened, you are relieved when a kindly-looking farmer steps out of the underbrush. But as you peer into the man's green-eyed face, you notice his brown, bark-like skin, his unusual lack of eyebrows, and the shaggy beard filled with twigs and leaves. This is not a man at all, but the deadly leshi—and he has you trapped.

The leshi, who serves as the protector of the forest, is a tricky, shapeshifting creature that kills travelers. It can shrink to the size of a single leaf or grow as tall as a tree. Its favorite disguise is a peasant farmer, but you can spot it by its lack of a shadow or eyebrows.

Every forest has its own leshi. It traps unsuspecting humans by using its magic to rearrange the forest around them. Other times, it lures travelers off the path by mimicking a familiar voice.

But as tricky as it can be, the leshi leaves most travelers alone—as long as they don't break the laws of the forest. So while you're in the woods, don't whistle, don't yell, and don't trample the foliage. The warning "Keep off the grass" takes on a whole new meaning with the leshi!

MERLIN MEMO If you want to trick the leshi (instead of the leshi tricking you), walk backward through the forest. It will not be able to follow your backward tracks, and you'll have it *barking* up the wrong tree.

TROLL

(TROL)

LOCATION: SCANDANAVIA

DANGER RATING: 💀💀

With their stone-colored skin, beady eyes, and scraggly hair filled with bird droppings, you'd hardly notice a troll standing silently amid the trees, waiting to ambush you! Trolls are famous for their dirty tricks, but, fortunately, they're easy to outwit.

Trolls are huge, grouchy creatures that live primarily underground in smelly caves—though some prefer the underside of a bridge. There are also mountain trolls, forest trolls, and water trolls. In Finland, there's an especially evil troll imprisoned under water by magic rune stones.

The most powerful trolls have two or three heads, and they're often the most irritable ones because their heads cannot get along. Some trolls can shapeshift, disguising themselves as rocks, logs, or animals, but many are too stupid to remember their own spells.

Trolls hate noise, and the sound of church bells repels them. They're also deathly afraid of lightning, since Thor the thunder god is one of their greatest enemies. If trolls come above ground during daylight, they turn to stone. Yet many are too dumb to remember this, which explains Scandinavia's many troll-shaped boulders.

MONSTER MESSAGE

Head #1: Hey, take that back! Trolls is not dumb.

Head #2: We is smart...and strong.

Head #1: I will crush whoever says so! Hand me the club!

Head #2: I don't have it! You have it!

Head #1: Liar! Give me the club!

(The troll's heads continue to argue until the sun comes up, and the troll is turned into stone.)

UNICORN
(YOO-NI-KORN)

LOCATION: NORTHERN AFRICA, THE MIDDLE EAST, AND INDIA

DANGER RATING: 💀

Standing at the edge of a clearing, you hold your breath as you see a unicorn emerge from the forest. Its silvery mane is flowing in the breeze, its horse body shimmers, and its single, pearly-white horn reflects the sun's rays.

The ultimate symbol of purity and beauty, the unicorn is the most elusive creature on earth. Infinitely gentle, the unicorn is also strong and fast, which makes capturing one almost impossible.

A unicorn must submit itself to capture, but only if the conditions are right. A pure maiden, dressed in her finest garments, must sit in a clearing. Drawn to her purity, the unicorn will approach without fear, kneel beside her, and place its head in her lap. When the maiden grasps the unicorn's horn, the beast is trapped and cannot escape until she releases it.

The horn of the unicorn, called an alicorn, is a prized possession since it extends its owner's life. The alicorn can also detect poisons, so powerful rulers often fashion their drinking cups from one.

Naysayers claim that these alicorns are really the horn from a narwhal. If a peddler attempts to sell you a unicorn's horn, test it by using it to draw a circle in the dirt. Then place a scorpion or spider within that circle. The horn's anti-poison power should keep the poisonous insect from leaving the circle.

CREATURE CONNECTION The Chinese unicorn is called a **KI-LIN**, and the sage Fu Hsi first saw it emerging from the Yellow River. It granted him the necessary knowledge to invent Chinese calligraphy. The Japanese unicorn, **SIN-YOU**, helped the sage Kau You judge important court cases. If the accused were guilty, the unicorn would run them through with its horn.

CREATURES OF SHADOW

When crypt doors creak and tombstones quake, you better beware! The shadow creatures are rising. They are the ones who go bump in the night and haunt your worst nightmares. You just may catch a glimpse of them in the moonlight, but only for a second before they slip back into the darkness that they call home.

MERLIN MEMO Who knows what creepies and crawlies lurk in the shadows? These creatures are the worst! I admit I was hunting them half-heartedly—hoping *not* to find them. Unfortunately, they started hunting me instead!

MY HUNT FOR THE YETI WAS ONE OF MY MORE CHILLING ADVENTURES.

ARTIC EXPEDITION

DON'T EVER ASK A ZOMBIE IF HE CAN GIVE YOU A HAND.

SILVER BULLET: BREAK GLASS IN CASE OF WEREWOLF ATTACK

BABA YAGA

(BAH-BUH YAH-GUH)

LOCATION: RUSSIA

DANGER RATING: 💀💀💀💀💀💀

In the darkest part of the woods stands a bizarre, little cottage on two chicken legs. If any unwanted guest tries to enter it, the cottage spins away from them. But who would want to go into such a place? Everyone knows it is the home of Baba Yaga.

With coarse, wiry hair, a bulging nose, warty skin, and iron teeth, Baba Yaga is an ogress witch, whose very name is too terrifying to speak in more than hushed tones. She practices ancient magic, and some say she knows the secret to immortality. Baba Yaga flies through the air in her giant mortar, using her pestle to steer. As she flies, a broom sweeps away all traces of her passage.

When wicked parents want to get rid of their children, they send them on an errand to Baba Yaga's cottage. The witch is happy to welcome these children to dinner—or more accurately, *to be* dinner. She stews them up and adds their bones to the skeletal fence that surrounds her yard. So beware if your parents ask you to run an errand to Baba Yaga's place!

In spite of her witchy ways, Baba Yaga has been a helper, too. Some children have outwitted her, and, in return, Baba Yaga has given them gifts for their cleverness. She has also assisted brave adventurers by presenting them with special items for their quests, like a magic mirror, an enchanted ring, or a self-swinging sword.

MERLIN MEMO Approach Baba Yaga's home at your own risk! She owns a pack of man-eating dogs, a crafty cat, and a talking gate that cries out when anyone tries to escape her chicken-footed dwelling. I barely escaped myself! I thought Baba Yaga wanted to eat me, but she actually wanted something worse—a date!

BANSHEE

(BAN-SHEE)

LOCATION: IRELAND

DANGER RATING: 💀💀

Y ou are staying in the Irish mansion of a rich relative, and somewhere out on the moors, someone is wailing. Awoken by the sound, you near the window of your guest room and gasp. A flowing, white form hovers over the lake. It is the banshee shrieking out her grim message: Death is coming soon to this household.

Renowned for its ghostly screams, the banshee is a dreaded spirit of the fairy world. It is her duty to foretell an imminent death with a cry so piercing that it can shatter glass. Each banshee is attached to a particular family, and her cry is heard throughout the countryside when a member of that family is about to die.

Some say that banshees appear in the form of mournful young women—their eyes red from weeping. As they shriek and wail, they comb their long hair with a silver comb. According to myth, a Banshee's clothing is often stained with the blood of the soon-to-be-deceased—a ghastly foreshadowing of what is to come. The next time you hear wailing coming from beyond the windowpane, listen carefully! Heed its warning and play it safe.

CREATURE CONNECTION: Another ghoul is the **DOPPELGANGER**, a creature that looks exactly like you. If you happen to see your doppelganger, it is a sign of bad things to come. According to one story, Abraham Lincoln saw his doppelganger's face reflected in the mirror next to his own—its face pale and sickly. Lincoln took this as a sign that he would be elected president twice but would not survive his second term. He was right!

CHUPACABRA

(CHOO-PUH-KAH-BRAH)

LOCATION: CENTRAL AND SOUTH AMERICA

DANGER RATING: 💀💀💀

Y ou're standing in a farmer's field. It's eerily quiet, and just ahead, you spot a whole herd of goats sprawled out on the dusty ground. Their skin is intact, but in their necks, you see twin puncture holes. The blood has been drained completely from them. What could explain this baffling mystery?

Meet the Chupacabra. Goats, horses, cows, and chickens all fall prey to the creepy killer-beast whose name means "the goat sucker." Witnesses describe it as a lizard-skinned creature with spikes running up and down its spine. Its face is a terror, with a forked tongue, fangs, glowing red eyes, and sharp teeth. It stands over its victims for just a split second before springing away like a kangaroo. Some even think that the creature has a basilisk-style power to render its victims immobile with its hypnotic stare, making it even easier to feed on them!

Momentarily, the mystery of the Chupacabra seemed to come to an end: A Texas rancher killed a monstrous-looking creature, which turned out to be a skeletal coyote that had lost its hair to disease. Many declared the case solved! But coyotes, sick or not, eat their prey—they don't suck their blood. That is why many people continue to believe the real Chupacabra is still out there—lying low in the darkness until its chance to strike again!

MERLIN MEMO If you'd like to protect yourself (and your goats) from this bloodsucking monster, carry a bright light. The Chupacabra's eyes are super sensitive, so put it in the spotlight and send this midnight creeper running.

KITSUNE

(KIT-SOO-NAY)

LOCATION: JAPAN

DANGER RATING: 💀💀💀💀

One of your friends has been acting strange ever since she arrived home from her family vacation in Japan. At lunch, she scarfed down her food (and everyone else's), licked her hands clean, and curled up on the floor for a nap. She looks strange, too. Her eyes seem beady and her ears are almost pointy.

The other day, you could have sworn you saw a fox tail pop out the back of her jacket—just for a split second. Watch out! Your friend is a kitsune in disguise!

Devilish and devious, the kitsune is a shapeshifting, fox-like creature with multiple tails. A young kitsune can take *almost* any shape. They can disguise themselves as other animals, grow as tall as a tree, or appear as a moon hanging in the sky. But only when they've reached 100 years of age can they take on human form. That's when they become especially dangerous—tricking and murdering their victims using familiar faces.

If people you know begin to look fox-like, develop a huge appetite, or run naked through the street, they may be a kitsune! When this happens, remember these tips: Even when disguised as a human, a kitsune still casts a fox-shaped shadow. They also have trouble hiding their tails, which keep popping out of their disguised forms. Look for these signs, and you might be able to out-fox the kitsune before it's too late!

MERLIN MEMO You can tell a kitsune's age by how many tails it has. The oldest kitsune, ones with nine tails, have lived for 1,000 years. Surviving so long, these kitsune are trickier than all the rest. I should know. Several of those old foxes gave me a walloping in chess.

ONI

(OH-NEE)

LOCATION: JAPAN

DANGER RATING: 💀💀💀

f the monster before you has three eyes, frightening horns, and an enormous mouth edged with tusks, you have come face to face with an oni. The oni are red-skinned ogres with incredible strength and malicious minds, who wear tiger-pelt loincloths and brandish deadly, spiked clubs to clobber their victims. In fact, the Japanese have a saying, "As deadly as an oni with an iron club," and rightfully so. Oni are known for using their supernatural powers to cause famine, disease, and even earthquakes.

Oni hordes ambush unsuspecting villages and carry off innocent victims to their hideouts. According to myth, the greatest adversary of the oni was the hero Momotaro, a warrior born from a magical peach. When the Oni King abducted villagers from the countryside, Momotaro made his way to the oni's island and defeated them with the help of his pet dog, a monkey, and a pheasant. Then he commanded the defeated oni to break off their horns, which transformed them into kindly spirits, and they did no more evil.

If you happen to spot a horned oni, you can be sure it is up to no good! Hopefully, you are traveling with some pet allies—like Momotaro was—and you can simply yell, "Sic 'em!"

CREATURE CONNECTION In Japan, people perform festivals to drive out the oni. They throw soybeans at people dressed in oni masks and shout, "Oni out! Luck in!" They also place oni-faced tiles on the edges of their roofs in hopes that the oni will drive away any other evil spirits.

VAMPIRE
(VAM-PY-ER)

LOCATION: TRANSYLVANIA AND EASTERN EUROPE

DANGER RATING: 💀💀💀💀💀

In a chilly crypt, a ghostly-pale corpse stirs, its eyes open, and it rises to feed upon the living. Vampires only emerge at night and must return to their coffins by daybreak, or they will crumble into ash when touched by the sun's first rays.

Those who have been bitten by a vampire wake in the morning feeling drained (literally) from twin puncture marks in their neck. But a vampire will seldom kill its victim. It returns to feed from the same source, so the longer it can keep its presence a secret, the better. When vampires' victims die, they become vampires themselves. One superstition states that a baby born with teeth, too much hair, or a missing finger or toe could become a vampire.

But fear not! Crucifixes, garlic, and holy water all repel the unholy creature. Since the vampire must return to its coffin each night, vampire hunters search nearby cemeteries for freshly dug graves, and open the coffins of suspected vampires. If the corpse's cheeks look rosy, the hunters have found their predator. The vampire's body must be decapitated, burned, or have a stake driven into its heart (or all three for good measure!). It should be buried at a crossroads to make doubly sure it will not return.

MERLIN MEMO Vlad the Impaler, a Transylvanian prince who impaled his enemies on spikes, was said to be the inspiration for **COUNT DRACULA**, the most famous vampire!

CREATURE CONNECTION The **ADZE** is a bloodsucking creature from Ghana that takes the form of a firefly, attacks children, and can transform its victims into zombie-like slaves. Tales from the Philippines tell of the **ASWANG**, a vampire-like creature that appears as an old woman with leathery wings to rob graves, feast on corpses, and prey on children.

WEREWOLF
(WEHR-WOLF)

LOCATION: EUROPE AND NORTH AMERICA

DANGER RATING: 💀💀💀💀

One night you're out for a quiet walk under the glow of a full moon. It's such a nice night until you see…him. Bathed in moonlight, a man howls and screams as his body makes a horrific transformation. His skin bristles into fur, his teeth lengthen into fangs, and his cries of pain morph into a long, unbroken howl.

Werewolf literally means "man-wolf," and these creatures are humans under a terrible curse. Under the light of a full moon, their bodies and minds transform into that of a beast. Some werewolves hunt upright like a human, but others run upon all fours. Their appetite is wolf-like as well, and they will prey upon their fellow human beings. As much as they may wish to, werewolves are powerless to stop the transformation, so they live in dread of the full moon.

There are many ways to become a werewolf. Some say sleeping out under the full moon, eating wolf meat, or putting on a wolf's skin will cause the change. Others say that it is caused by a magical curse. This curse renders werewolves almost invincible, so the only way to kill one is to use a silver bullet or a silver-tipped arrow shot straight into the heart.

Since there are werewolves among us, watch for humans who have wolf-like eyes, extended canine teeth, or wild, bushy eyebrows that trail up their foreheads.

CREATURE CONNECTION   Indigenous tribes, such as the Navajo, tell stories of **SKIN-WALKERS**—warriors who can transform into animals at will. Some of their favorite shapes are bears, coyotes, foxes, and, of course, wolves. Many Mesoamerican stories feature shamans who can morph into jaguars.

YETI
(YEH-TEE)

LOCATION: TIBET, NEPAL, AND THE HIMALAYA MOUNTAINS

DANGER RATING: 💀

Half-blinded by snow, you climb higher into the Himalaya Mountains—higher than any explorer has ever gone. Yet as you trudge through the deepening banks, you see a stunning sight in the snow: a fresh, humanoid footprint—far larger than a human's can be. You are on the trail of the Yeti.

The Yeti looks like a giant, muscular ape, standing between 7-10 feet tall with brown, gray, or completely white hair. Yeti tracks have been found as high as 20,000 feet by many explorers, including the first to reach the peak of Mount Everest, Sir Edmund Hillary and Tenzing Norgay. The mountain people cultures in Tibet call the Yeti "human-like bear of the snow," which was mistranslated into English as "the Abominable Snowman."

The term "abominable" is harsh since the Yeti is typically not hostile to humans. Some say there are many yeti. Although they wander in snowy altitudes, they live in small groups amidst the alpine forests just below the snow line, where they eat frogs and small rodents. In yeti tribes the females are the leaders. Yeti mostly emerge at night, and you're more likely to hear one than see one, because they have a high-pitched screech that echoes through the mountains. They are also said to have their own language.

The people who live within the mountainous regions have utmost respect for the Yeti, and some stories say that when the mountain itself is angry with them, it will send out the Yeti to punish them.

CREATURE CONNECTION The Yeti is similar to the North American **SASQUATCH** or **BIGFOOT.** Both creatures are tall, ape-like, shy, and known for their impressive footprints. In Australian Aboriginal legends, the **YOWIE** is a savage ape-man with reddish-brown fur.

ZOMBIE

(ZOM-BEE)

LOCATION: CENTRAL AND WEST AFRICA, HAITI

DANGER RATING: 💀💀💀💀

A bony arm thrusts itself through the earth of a freshly dug grave. A skull-like face with an eerie grin and a ragged torso quickly follow. The grave can no longer hold this zombie. Its master has called it forth to do his bidding.

A zombie is a corpse that has been magically brought back to life. Stripped of its soul, the zombie has no will of its own and exists as the mere puppet of its master. Sorcerers in Africa were the first to dig up bodies and bewitch them into a state of living death. People who haven't died can also become zombies. A drug made from the poison of pufferfish hypnotizes victims into obedience.

A young African man once discovered that someone had disturbed his recently-deceased brother's grave. Suspecting magic, he hid in the graveyard and watched in shock as his brother rose from the grave and walked to a nearby farm, where a moonlit field full of the undead worked silently. The farm's owner, a notorious sorcerer, had bewitched an army of zombies to work his land.

The African slave trade carried the knowledge of zombies to Haiti, where belief in Bokors, or zombie-creating sorcerers, continues. The curse of living death resembles the horrific life endured by slaves in Haiti.

MERLIN MEMO A zombie may seem unstoppable, but if it eats salt or glimpses the sea, it will return to its grave. If you have a face-off with one, slyly suggest a salty, seaside snack.

CREATURE CONNECTION The Norse people speak of **DRAUGR**, corpses of Viking warriors that rise to attack the living, protecting their buried hordes of weapons from would-be looters.

CREATURES FROM BEYOND OUR WORLD

Each and every earthly creature, as strange and fantastic as it may be, is still familiar in some way. But what about creatures that live beyond our world, where the same rules do not apply? These are shifting and strange realms where life and death blur, and where spirit and body are no longer joined. Be careful! When visitors from different worlds step into our own, they may be here to invite you to journey back with them across the divide.

MERLIN MEMO: Traveling between this world and the next raises many questions—mainly "What should I pack?" The answer? Plenty of bribes for the guardians of these lands of death and darkness.

ANUBIS GAVE ME THIS WONDERFUL GIFT...OR AT LEAST I THOUGHT IT WAS WONDERFUL UNTIL I OPENED IT.

I WOULDN'T DARE GO INTO THE UNDERWORLD WITHOUT A DOGGY TREAT FOR CERBERUS. OR MAKE THAT THREE DOGGY TREATS... ONE FOR EACH HEAD.

Num-Num

Num-Nums

I RAN INTO A GENIE AND USED TWO OF MY WISHES, BUT I SAVED THE THIRD FOR LATER.

Good for 1 Wish

ANUBIS
(UH-NOO-BIS)

LOCATION: EGYPT

DANGER RATING: 💀

A shadowy man with the long snout and pointed ears of a jackal holds a human heart in his hands. This is Anubis, the protector of the dead. He places the heart tenderly upon a golden set of scales. On the opposite side, he places a single feather. The heart is a heavy one—weighed down by greed and selfishness. The tray containing it begins to sink.

Another shadow watches this hungrily from the darkness: **AMMIT** the devourer, a creature with the long jaws and crooked teeth of a crocodile, the front legs of a lion, and the haunches of a hippopotamus. The heart has failed the test, so Anubis picks it up and flings it to Ammit who does her duty: She gobbles it up.

Anubis has the head of a jackal, a desert scavenger dog known for digging up bodies shallowly buried in the sand. His fur coat is jet-black to resemble the discolored skin of a mummified body. In fact, it was clever Anubis who invented the art of mummification.

In the Egyptian land of the dead, it is Anubis's duty to judge the hearts of the deceased by weighing them against the Feather of Truth. Souls that pass the test enter into the afterlife. Those that fail have their very existence devoured by Ammit.

CREATURE CONNECTION In ancient Egypt, workers wearing Anubis masks removed a dead person's main organs and placed them in clay jars. Soaking the body in a special solution to preserve it, they then wrapped it in long strips of linen to create a mummy. Little statues of Anubis guard the mummy in its tomb—warning trespassers to beware the watchman of the dead.

CERBERUS
(SER-BER-US)

LOCATION: THE UNDERWORLD

DANGER RATING: 💀💀💀💀💀

Imagine for a moment that you are adventuring in ancient Greece. What began as a mountain cave is leading you deep into the earth—deeper than most mortals dare to venture. Soon you will cross the threshold into Hades, the land of the dead—or at least you will try. Six glowing eyes appear in the cavern ahead as the grim guardian of the Underworld blocks your path.

Three vicious dog heads snap and snarl on a single body and a twisting mane of live snakes strike and hiss—Cerberus is the ultimate guard dog. His duty is to decimate any mortal who attempts to enter the Underworld.

For Cerberus, three heads are better than one because he can see—and smell—in three different directions. His living snake tail also provides him with another set of devilish eyes. Even Cerberus's saliva is deadly. Where it falls to the earth, a poisonous plant, Aconite, springs up.

Luckily for you, this dog is fond of treats. So if you journey into Hades, come prepared with a special snack, or the snapping jaws of Cerberus will be the last sight you see!

MERLIN MEMO Only a handful of heroes have ever gotten past Cerberus alive. Psyche, a Greek princess, tricked the dog by tossing it a single sweet cake, which the three heads fought over fiercely while she shimmied by. Orpheus, the famous musician, charmed the dog with his enchanting music. And Hercules used his brute strength to wrestle the dog into submission. That's pretty good for heroes who weren't trained by yours truly.

DULLAHAN, THE GRIM REAPER, AND CHARON THE BOATMAN
(DOO-LUH-HAN, KAR-ON)

LOCATION: THE LAND OF THE DEAD

DANGER RATING: 💀💀💀💀💀💀💀💀💀💀

A skull-faced figure stands in the darkness as the wind catches his tattered robe. In his bony hands he carries an hourglass and a scythe. The hourglass tells him that the sands of a mortal's life have run out, and with one quick swipe, the scythe severs the mortal's spirit from his body.

Death is a fate that awaits all mortals, and the **Grim Reaper** is just one personification of this inevitable event. Many cultures around the world have their own messenger of death—each as creepy as the last.

In Ireland, people speak of a headless horseman, the **Dullahan.** Under his arm, he carries his severed head—smiling from ear to ear. In his other hand, a whip made from a human spine, which he uses to lash out the eyes of any who witness his midnight ride. He will only speak one word: the name of the person who is to die. Sometimes he drives a carriage called the Death Coach, made from human bones and pulled by headless horses, with two burning skulls for headlights. When its doors open, you must enter.

In the Greek underworld, **Charon the Boatman** stands between life and death. The recently deceased stand on the cold banks of the River Styx, the barrier to the Underworld, waiting for passage on Charon's ferryboat. Any soul can climb aboard by paying the toll. But in order to pay, their family must have buried them with a coin in their mouth. Souls who don't have a coin remain stranded between life and death.

CREATURE CONNECTION The Dullahan is one possible inspiration for the **HEADLESS HORSEMAN**, the legendary ghost that haunts the village of Sleepy Hollow.

GENIE

(JEE-NEE)

LOCATION: THE MIDDLE EAST

DANGER RATING: 💀💀💀

Walking along the beach, you find an old oil lamp in the sand. There seems to be ancient writing on it, so you rub off some of the grime with your sweatshirt. Suddenly, smoke streams out and an enormous genie takes shape above you. You might think he will grant you three wishes, but genies are not always friendly wish-granters. In fact, most of them are trapped for a reason, and releasing them could have deadly consequences! So summon them at your own peril.

Genies (or djinn) are powerful creatures. They can appear as humans, cats, ostriches, dogs, snakes, and outright monsters. Formed from two elements, fire and wind, genies possess power over nature and can cause natural disasters like whirlwinds and sandstorms. They inhabit a realm between earth and the heavens and emerge to wreak havoc on the world. Wise men have captured genies and trapped them inside bottles, oil lamps, and magic rings. Iron can bind a genie, and once shackled, they must do whatever their masters require.

Once, a poor fisherman found an ancient bottle and released the genie inside. But instead of thanking him for this deed, the genie decided to kill him. The fisherman only survived by using his quick wits: He asked the genie to prove that a being as large and powerful as him could really fit inside a tiny bottle. To prove himself, the genie shrank back into his bottle, and the fisherman quickly plugged it shut and hurled it back into the sea.

MERLIN MEMO If you encounter a disagreeable genie, try to trick it back into its bottle. Then put a cork in it. On the other hand, if you encounter an agreeable genie, it will be everything you ever wished for!

GOLEM
(GOL-UM)

LOCATION: PRAGUE

DANGER RATING: 💀💀

It's late at night, and you know you're supposed to be in bed. But you are curious what the rabbi, the Jewish teacher you serve, is up to. You climb the stairs to the attic and crack the door to see inside. The rabbi is putting the finishing touches on his creation: a massive human form shaped from clay. The figure is lifeless—for now. The rabbi rolls up a piece of parchment that contains mystic letters, opens the clay man's lips, and places the parchment roll inside. The figure trembles, and its earthen eyes crack open—shining with an unearthly light.

A golem is a human-shaped being made from clay. Golem means "raw material" in Hebrew. The creature is larger and stronger than an ordinary man, but remains lifeless until magic awakens it. This can be done with a secret combination of Hebrew letters written on its forehead or on a sheet of paper placed in its mouth.

Certain rabbis studied the Hebrew alphabet for years—searching for just the right combination of letters that could bestow life. At last, a rabbi discovered the secret. The rabbi commanded the golem to do only good deeds—serving its master faithfully. It did so at first, but soon it developed a mind of its own and set fire to the entire city before the rabbi was able to stop it.

MERLIN MEMO A golem is incredibly strong and invulnerable to attack, so the only way to defeat one is to remove the Hebrew letters from its body. Then it will crumble into dust.

HELA
(HEL-UH)

LOCATION: SCANDANAVIA

DANGER RATING: 💀💀💀💀💀💀

A dark throne rises above you, and a woman sits upon it. One side of her body is that of a living woman. The other side is a grossly decaying corpse. Life and death exist side by side on Hela, the Norse goddess of death. This is her kingdom: the frozen netherworld of Niflheim, where the souls of the dishonorable dead reside. While the souls of warriors who die in battle rise to the hall of Valhalla, those who die from sickness or old age descend to Hela. There they live a silent, cold existence and await the end of time.

Hela is the daughter of the trickster god, Loki, the enemy of the other Norse gods. Because of Hela's vile nature, Odin, the All-Father of the Gods, banished her to rule over the dead, but in Niflheim her power grew and grew until not even Odin could overpower her. At the end of time, she will gain her revenge. Loki will command her to awaken the dead, and together they will lead an army of deathless warriors against the gods. This battle is Ragnarok, and it will destroy the world. Almost all of the gods will die. Although Hela and her allies will think they have won, a new world will emerge—a better, more peaceful world born from the ashes of the old.

CREATURE CONNECTION Hela has two brothers who are just as monstrous as she is: **JORMUNGAND**, a killer serpent long enough to surround the entire world, and **FENRIR**, a wolf so massive that his open jaws scrape the sky.

JERSEY DEVIL
(JER-ZEE DEV-IL)

LOCATION: NEW JERSEY, USA

DANGER RATING: 💀💀💀

I n 1735, a poor woman named Mother Leeds learned that she would soon bear her thirteenth child. Her family could not afford another mouth to feed, so rather than reacting with joy, she shouted, "Let it be a devil!" She would live to regret these words.

The child was born normally enough, but soon transformed into something terrifying. Horns sprouted out of the baby's tender scalp, wings budded from its back, and a devil-like tail grew from its tailbone. As the family looked on with horror, its face lengthened into a horse's snout, and its feet hardened into hooves. The devilish creature flew at its mother—tearing out her throat with its sharp teeth. The rest of the family tried to flee, but the creature ripped them limb from limb before flying up the chimney and disappearing into the nearby cedar swamp.

For over 300 years, thousands of people reported seeing the Jersey Devil in the Pine Barrens swamp. Its inhuman howls rise out above the trees, and campers brave enough to stay there catch glimpses of it in the moonlight. Hunters spot its tracks in the snow, but their dogs refuse to follow the scent. Farmers report massacred livestock as proof that the Jersey Devil still hunts its prey.

CREATURE CONNECTION A New Jersey school offered a free canoe trip for students who received good grades. But something went horribly wrong. Their field trip was near the spot that the Jersey Devil haunts. To the students' horror, the creature stalked their canoes downriver—growling at them from the riverbank. Scared out of their wits, they left that place swearing that they had barely escaped the infamous devil.

THE MOTHMAN
(MOTH-MAN)

LOCATION: WEST VIRGINIA, USA

DANGER RATING: 💀💀

Your family is driving along a familiar highway when suddenly your dad brings the car to a screeching halt. A tall, winged man with large, red eyes is standing in the glow of the car's headlights. With a flurry of his wings, the creature shoots straight up into the air, and your dad slams on the gas. As the car speeds away, relief washes over your family until you realize the glowing red eyes have returned—this time in the rearview mirror.

With its enormous, hypnotic eyes and huge, bird-like wings, the Mothman's nightmarish features struck terror into the residents of Point Pleasant, West Virginia. For thirteen months beginning in 1966, over 100 people reported seeing the Mothman. Some witnesses said the creature chased their car and matched its speed—even at 100 miles an hour—before vanishing into thin air.

The Mothman's reign of terror was accompanied by other oddities: Strange lights flashing in the sky and suited agents called "men in black" asking questions around town. The hysteria came to a head when the Silver Bridge, connecting West Virginia to Ohio, came crashing down, killing 46 people. Since witnesses had reported seeing the Mothman on the bridge days before, some folks said he was responsible for the catastrophe. Others wondered if he had been a visitor from another world trying to warn them. After this tragedy the Mothman sightings stopped, and the creature simply disappeared.

CREATURE CONNECTION Some say the Mothman was an alien. Others say he was a spirit conjured up long ago by an indigenous Shawnee chief who put a curse on the town of Point Pleasant. Skeptics say Mothman was just a barn owl and a lot of imagination.

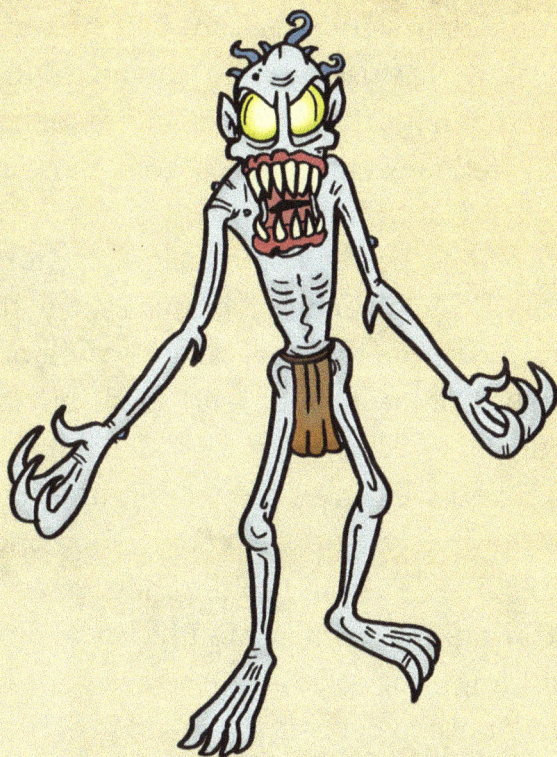

WENDIGO

(WEN-DEE-GO)

LOCATION: NORTH AMERICA

DANGER RATING: 💀💀💀💀💀

Lanky and gaunt with long, branch-like arms and claws, the wendigo jumps from one treetop to another, scanning the frozen forest below for signs of life. Its lips are cracked and bloodied—sliced open by the constant gnashing of its needle-like teeth. It hungers for human flesh, which is unsettling, because this creature used to be a human itself.

Many indigenous tribes, among them the Algonquin people, tell tales of the wendigo, describing it as a creature taller than a human and bone-thin from hunger. When people become so desperately hungry that they eat the flesh of another human, they transform into a wendigo. From this time on, they will only crave human flesh. They will feed and feed, but they will never be filled.

The wendigo welcomes the winter, and its hunting ground is the lonely, snow-covered woodlands. Fearing for their lives, people huddle indoors as much as possible during the winter months to avoid a gory death. But hungry people have to leave their houses at some point—only to become the wendigo's prey.

The wendigo serves as a warning: No matter how horrible hunger becomes, do not resort to cannibalism. Better to lose your life than lose your soul.

CREATURE CONNECTION The wendigo is similar to the werewolf (page 99), a cursed creature that goes wild for the taste of human flesh.

JOURNEY'S END

So our journey through a world of fantastic creatures is drawing to a close. Conquering all the creatures in this book is no small feat, but you have risen to the challenge. Along the way, I hope you've seen mythical creatures for what they are: creative reflections of the real world.

But don't think this is the end. Another journey awaits you. Use the creativity of these creatures to inspire you to see your world with fresh eyes. Let the same curiosity and courage you experienced here carry you on to new adventures!

If you are interested in learning more about mythical creatures, there are still more resources in the back of this book. Use them to guide your learning and lead you further on.

MERLIN MEMO After traveling around the world, I finally discovered some of my favorite creatures of all—the "creature comforts" of home! It's been wonderful adventuring with you, and I wish you all the best. Never stop wondering and exploring. Onward! Ever onward!

CREATURE INDEX

RECOMMENDED READING

Children's Book of Mythical Beasts and Magical Monsters. Edited by Deborah Lock. London: DK Press, 2018.

Connolly, Kieron, and Gerrie McCall. *Dragons: Fearsome Monsters from Myth and Fiction.* New York: Scholastic, 2013.

Drake, Edward. *Monsterology.* Edited by Dugald A. Steer. Somerville, MA: Candlewick Press, 2008.

Hamby, Zachary. *The Hero's Guidebook: Creating Your Own Hero's Journey.* Ava, MO: Creative English Teacher Press, 2019.

Lawrence, Sarah. *The Atlas of Monsters: Mythical Creatures from Around the World.* New York: Running Press Kids, 2019.

Sautter, A.J. *Field Guide to Griffins, Unicorns, and Other Mythical Beasts.* Makato, MN: Capstone Press, 2014.

REFERENCES

Borges, Jorge Luis. *The Book of Imaginary Creatures.* London: Penguin, 1970.

Capper, D.S. "The Friendly Yeti." *Journal for the Study of Religion, Nature, and Culture,* 6, no. 1 (2012): 71-87.

Cotterell, Arthur and Rachel Storm. *The Ultimate Encyclopedia of Mythology.* London: Hermes House, 2006.

Funk and Wagnalls Standard Dictionary of Folklore, Mythology, and Legend. Ed. Maria Leach. New York: Funk and Wagnalls, 1972.

Griffis, William Elliot. *Dutch Fairy Tales for Young People*. Project Gutenberg, 2003. http://www.gutenberg.org/files/7871/7871-h/7871-h.htm

Lyons, Stephen. "The Legend of Loch Ness." *PBS*, 1999. https://www.pbs.org/wgbh/nova/article/legend-loch-ness/

Matthews, Caitlin and John. *The Element Encyclopedia of Magical Creatures*. New York: Harper Element, 2005.

Moran, Mark, and Mark Sceurman. *Weird New Jersey*. New York: Sterling, 2009.

Mythical Monsters. Chris McNab, editor. New York: Scholastic, 2006.

Myths and Legends: An Illustrated Guide to their Origins and Meanings. London: DK, 2019.

Rosen, Brenda. *The Mythical Creatures Bible*. New York: Sterling, 2009.

Sandburg, Carl. *Abraham Lincoln: The Prairie Years*. New York: Harcourt, Brace and Co., 1926.

"The Thunderbird Symbol." *Spirits of the West Coast Art Gallery*, 2019. www.spiritsofthewestcoast.com

Tripp, Edward. *The Meridian Handbook of Classical Mythology*. New York: Meridian, 1970.

Warner, Elizabeth. *Russian Myths*. Austin, TX: University of Texas Press, 2002.

ACKNOWLEDGEMENTS

Throughout this process, I have tried to write the type of book that would have sparked my own imagination at a young age, and I hope I have been successful in that.

I am grateful to four authors, J.R.R. Tolkien, C.S. Lewis, Ursula K. Le Guin, and Lloyd Alexander, for showing me how fantasy worlds can teach valuable lessons about life and its meaning.

I would like to thank my parents, who from an early age taught me to cultivate creativity and use it to better others.

I am thankful to my children, Luke and Jane, who were the perfect ages to serve as sample readers of this book, and did so willingly. And another special thanks to Luke for helping me with the many illustrations in this book.

As always, I would like to thank Rachel—my editor, my supporter, my wife, my friend.

And, most of all, I would like to thank God for giving his creations the power of creation themselves.

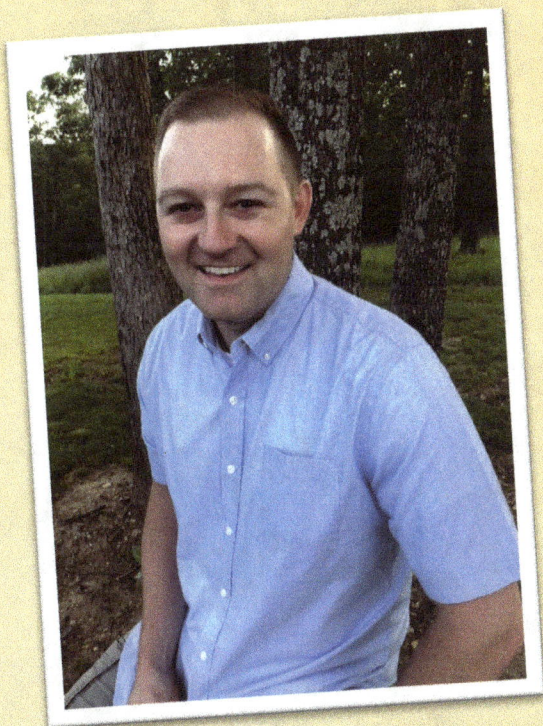

Zachary Hamby is an English teacher in rural Missouri. Being a lifelong fan of myth and legend, he loves teaching young people about ancient heroes and fantastic creatures. He has written and illustrated the *Reaching Olympus* series, the *Mythology for Teens* series, *The Hero's Guidebook*, and *Introduction to Mythology for Kids*. He resides in the Ozarks with his wife, Rachel (also an English teacher), and their two children, Luke and Jane.

For more information about Zachary visit his website www.creativeenglishteacher.com or contact him by email at **zachary@creativeenglishteacher.com**

www.ingramcontent.com/pod-product-compliance
Lightning Source LLC
Chambersburg PA
CBHW070808280326
41934CB00012B/3112